Also by Charles Cantalupo

POETRY

Sykes in Eritrea

The Woodstock Sandal and Further Steps

Where War Was

Light the Lights

Anima/l Wo/man and Other Spirits

The Art of Hope

NONFICTION

Mandated Massacres: Ethiopian Policy in Eritrea, 1961-1991

Non-Native Speaker: Selected and Sundry Essays

War and Peace in Contemporary Eritrean Poetry

Poetry, Mysticism, and Feminism:"from th' nave to the chops"

Ngũgĩ wa Thiong'o: Texts and Contexts

The World of Ngũgĩ wa Thiong'o

A Literary Leviathan: Thomas Hobbes's Masterpiece of Language

TRANSLATION

Our Village: Poems by Tesfamariam Woldemariam

Who Needs a Story? Contemporary Eritrean Poetry in Tigrinya, Tigre and Arabic

We Invented the Wheel: Poems by Reesom Haile

We Have Our Voice: Selected Poems of Reesom Haile

MEMOIR

Joining Africa: from Anthills to Asmara

FILM

Against All Odds: African Languages and Literatures into the 21st Century

Clooscape the Poet

Charles Cantalupo

SPUYTEN DUYVIL
NEW YORK CITY

Contents

PREFACE

Clooscape the Poet retells stories about Koluskap, the most familiar and renowned figure in the Wabanaki oral tradition. Variants of his name include Gluskap, Kluscap, Kluskap, Kuloskap, Klooscap, Clooscap, Cloos Crumpo, Clote Scarp, Kloskomba, Klosekurbeh, Glooscap, Glooskap, Gloskap, Glous'gap, Glusgehbeh, Gluskabe, Gluskab, Gluscabe, Gluskabi, Gluscapi, Gloosecap, and more, now including Clooscape.

The Wabanaki people consist of the Abenaki, Mi'kmaq, Maliseet, Passamaquoddy, and Penobscot nations. They live throughout northern New England, especially Maine, and Eastern Canada. They have a long history, being among the First Peoples, indigenous to North America.

For all the variations of the name, Koluskap, even more variations make up the stories of his life. Retellings are legion and so are their contents and styles: oral (whether or not transcribed) or written, contemporary and/or historical, verse and prose, in their original languages or in translation, of which there are many, too. Epithets and terms to define him also vary widely: including clown-like, cultural hero, Creator, deceiver, demigod, divinity, friend of man, fairy tale, bedtime story, a living tradition, god, god-man, great chief, hero, hunter, legend, land shaper, lord of men and beasts, Lord of Light, like Hiawatha, like Jesus, like Moses, like Noah, like Odin, like Thor, like an Indian Prometheus, magician, doctor, medicine man, maker of rules, man, master, *motewolon* (Passamaquoddy word for person with spiritual powers), a new Arion, Aryan-like, prophet, prophecy, protector, self-created, savior, shaman, solar hero, spirit, spirit-helper, teacher, transformer, trickster, twin, warrior, and liar. Literally, the name, Koluskap, with spelling variants, means "liar" in the Maliseet, Penobscot, and Passamaquoddy languages, but the connotation is not malevolent. For example, he lies to save his life when his enemies, including his brother, want to kill him.

Yet in *Clooscape the Poet*, he is a storyteller. In fact, he is the source of what has become a canon of traditional tales and legends about him: retold time and time again in a myriad of ways and presenting him in a multiplicity of roles. The stories originate in Clooscape's mind as memories, observations, visions, fantasies, dreams, and delusions. He is the author of himself, amazed and enamored with his Wabanaki homeland. What others in their retellings will make out of him – to entertain, to teach, to uplift, to inspire, to protect, to identify – becomes their storytelling, too. However vainly, Clooscape even intimates and hopes for such an outcome, as might any author. Yet with all his art of self-expression and self-enhancement – a primary purpose of any art – he remains acutely aware of being mundane and inescapably mortal: in his words, "a man with a wife and child" who "lived near a stream."

Clooscape the Poet draws on the many retellings and translations of Koluskap stories, but none of them derives from an original and authoritative oral or print source. The earliest print versions go back to the second half of the nineteenth century. Oral versions of the stories, from which the earliest as well as later print versions of the stories derive, go back farther – conterminous, perhaps, with Wabanaki history and pre-history or parts thereof.

Not that a comparison or collation of all or as many as possible of the Koluskap narratives could ever lead to establishing a single or corrected text. They vary too much. There can be no one version of his birth, life, or death. Within such an expansive storytelling tradition, a typical account might reiterate any of its standard details and developments while adding something different.

The assortment of names and roles attributed to Koluskap as well as the variety of its sources and retellings generate contrast, collision, and collage. As a fusion of such multifarious characterizations in previous retellings, Clooscape becomes, in well-known words from Shakespeare's *A Midsummer Night's Dream*, "The lunatic, the lover and the poet." He has "The poet's eye, in a fine frenzy rolling." He

...glance[s] from heaven to earth, from earth to heaven;

And as imagination bodies forth

The forms of things unknown, the poet...

Turns them to shapes and gives to airy nothing

A local habitation and a name.

Taking the form of a poem written in English, *Clooscape the Poet* has a precedent in *Kuloskap the Master and Other Algonkin Poems* (1902), "Translated Metrically," as stated on the title page by Charles Godfrey Leland (1824-1903) and John Dyneley Prince (1868-1945). Leland and Prince also drew off a wide variety of sources, whom Leland listed as "Authorities" in an earlier work, *The Algonquin Legends of New England* or *Myths and Folk Lore of the Micmac, Passamaquoddy, and Penobscot Tribes* (1884). These sources included his Passamaquoddy contemporaries, the great governor and visual artist, Tomah Joseph (1837-1914), and the indomitable legislator and linguist, Lewis Mitchell (1847-1930). Additionally, a prodigious array of native informers and seminal scholars helped Leland and Prince in their work. *Clooscape the Poet* springs from Leland, Prince, and their distinguished company as well as well as from the many translations, scholarly and critical analyses of Koluskap narratives ever since.

Leland wrote in 1884 that when he first heard the Koluskap stories, "The old people declared that they had heard from their progenitors that all of these stories were once sung; that they themselves remembered when many of them were poems" (1884:3). In 1758, Abbe Pierre Maillard, a French priest who created a system for writing Mi'kmaq language, recorded that when he spoke with Mi'kmaq, "I ... take care of observing measure and cadence in the delivery of my words.... As nothing enchants those people more than a style of metaphors and allegories" (1758:2-3).

Leland also wrote that after many decades of writing in Europe and

America, he was "awakened by a spell which he never felt in other lands" when he first came to the land of the Wabanaki. Same with me. He also found "that every hill and dale...had its romantic legend, its beautiful poem, or its marvellous myth" that was "verified" in the vast collection of these traditions" that "still" survived (1902:14-15). So did I.

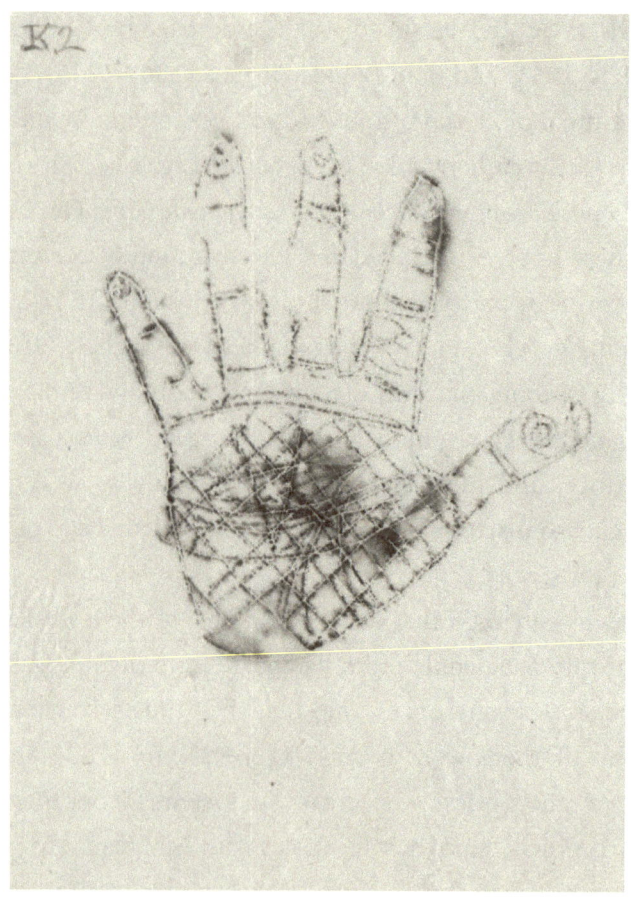

CLOOSCAPE THE POET

"How do you want to be born," I asked my twin brother, Malsum.
Still in the womb I accepted coming out the normal way
Into the light, but then he refused to wait. "I'll birth myself."
Right after me, he broke through my mother's ribs and left her dead.
How we survived, just the two of us together I don't know.
Some kind of magic or mystery was keeping us alive.
Deep in the dark woods the ferns would make me think how I could die.
As did my brother cry over cattails swaying in the streams.
Or so he said when I asked him if he ever thought of death.
He had already asked me the question, and I lied to him,
Since I remembered our mother. So, I said, "Feather's softness."
Discontent, thinking he knew best, self-obsessed, and destructive:
He hadn't changed since birth. Yet the world back then was just like him.
As I was sleeping one night, I woke up, drowning in feathers.
Choking and seeing my brother, I should not have been surprised,
But I was mad, and I chased him down to where the cattails grew.
Grabbing a bunch of them, I began to whip him, and he laughed.
Next thing I saw him dead – reeds pulled tightly, digging in his neck.
Waking again but to cry and sing for him, I went back home.
My name is Clooscape, and I'm a poet. Malsum's name means wolf.

Separate birth from death, brother from his brother
One gently born and one bursting through his mother
Ferns in the dark woods and cattails in the streams
Choking on feathers and waking from bad dreams
Hated and angry, unworthy and unruled
Who kills whom first depends on not being fooled

Lightning snapped into some grains of metal in a mound of sand
Like I had made myself out of need and spirit pinned to shore.
Flat on my back as my arms formed north and south, I couldn't move.
Like a first child of the sunrise in my face and outstretched west,
I became conscious the way a very heavy stone can float.
"What am I doing here?" I remembered. Lightning snapped the shore.
I killed my brother and had been born before. I could get up.
Next to me I had a bow and arrows, and I realized why.
Shooting one into an ash tree, I saw people burst from it.
Shooting one into the air, I saw it raining animals.
People like animals, animals like people – and the same.
I shot again when I saw them transform into each other.
"What am I doing?" I asked myself. Am I the one who made
Rivers run one way down, oceans with their tides always moving
High or low? How about fire not only burning but put out?
Who leads the wind I can only follow, face, or head into?
What I create seems like so much less than what I can destroy.
Caught between such extremes when I'm blown away what have I changed,
If I can't clear the streams, give things names, change evil into stone,
Pass through impassable mountains, rest, and meet somebody soon?

Sand and need　　　　　*Spirit from death*
Nothing moves　　　　　*Lightning strikes*
I make myself　　　　　*And look for more*
Dawn kisses me　　　　　*So I have eyes*
The four directions　　　*Spread me out*
Where to go　　　　　　*What to do*
Unknown shore　　　　　*Been here before*
Brother I killed　　　　*He'd kill me*
Arrow hits tree　　　　*People pour out*
Arrow in air　　　　　*Raining animals*
People and animals　　　*Looking the same*
More arrows fly　　　　*What am I doing*
Rivers run　　　　　　*One way down*
Tides nonstop　　　　　*Work the fire*
Who leads the wind　　*Where to go*
What I create　　　　　*Less than destroy*
Blown away　　　　　　*What I've changed*
Clear the streams　　　*Give things names*
Evil to stone　　　　　*Impassable pass*
Rest and again　　　　*Not alone*

Every way out looked dark but my sunrise re-awakening
Made it light where my canoe of granite and water pointed,
As if becoming one island and afloat unto ourselves:
Finally unlashed from the masts of spruces, pines, and white birches;
At forty-five degrees from the North Pole and the equator;
Passamaquoddy and Cobscook Bays both sucking on my tongue,
So hard my doubts disappeared in clouds of salt air and balsam.
Cliffs amethysted and jasper rattling shores demanded, "Land."
Power to make water turn around and then flow back again,
Yet to extremes, might have carried me this far, but the moment

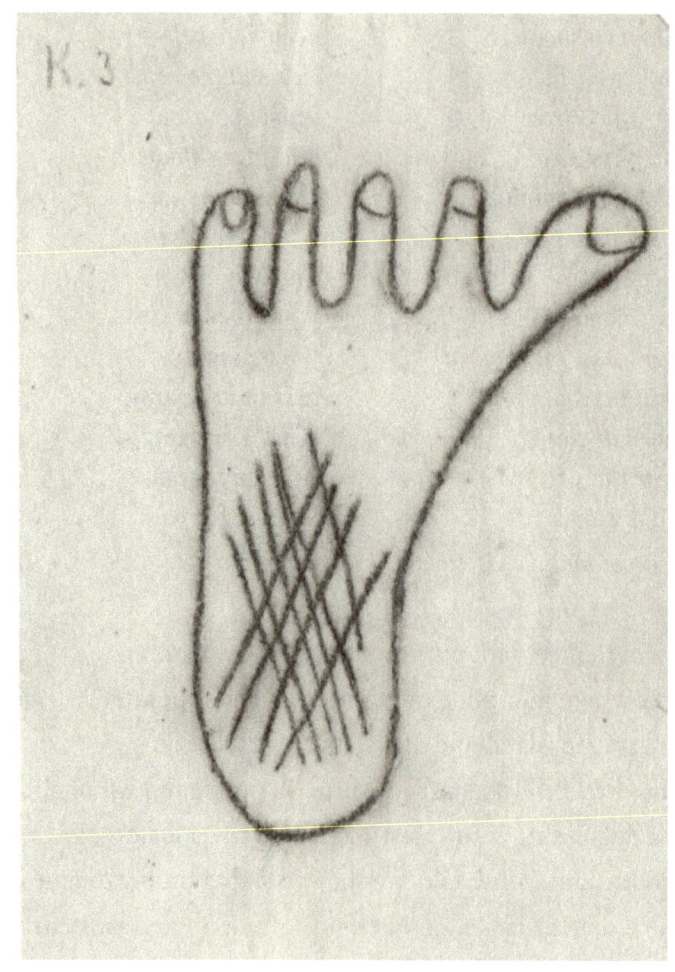

Made me feel twice as big, twice as strong, and twice the soul or else
Bad currents, deadly falls, crushing rocks, and non-stop freezing cold
Like living monsters would wipe out every home, including mine:
Not if my handprints had marked them, as I did, come from nothing.
All the more I should feel driven, but it felt like a return.
Back to the woman I learned from. She could simply wash her face
And be adorned. She could be part turtle, bear, and caribou.
Back to a child like a sable made of music to be saved.
Back to my messengers, wolves – and back surrounded by my loons
Calling in need, "Clooscape, Clooscape," and the nodding pines like grass.

> *Back in the dawn*
> *Sailing the land*
> *Speaking the sea*
> *Inside me*

> *No more cares*
> *Or alone*
> *Than the loons*
> *Calling my name*

Less and less coming and going here: I would stay longer.
Person to person and animal to animal equal
Gave way to fighting to be the master continually.
Torture and blood that no man or woman or their child survived:
Learned from the animals since they had to be the masters first.
Not anymore. So what if a pretty squirrel I was petting
Swelled to three times my size and clawed down a tree on top of me.
So what if once the moose let me stroke its antlers one minute
And the next tossed me down so I could be stomped into a pulp.
So what if shyness of beavers only wanted to drown me.
On my own I learned the basics, and I knew how to react.
Prey or be preyed upon. "Meat! Forget your vegetables," she said.
Lying in bed, I was dreaming "I'll go hunting" like a song.

Why use a porcupine quill and deerskin game bag anymore?
Give me the one that I wove from her hair for the woods this time.
I'll call the animals. "All of you, get out here or you'll die!
This is the end of the world. The sun's a goner. Come to me."
Rabbits, racoons, foxes, woodchucks, bears – you name it they appeared.
"Jump in my bag. You'll be safe, and you'll survive. Jump in my bag."
Everyone did, and I tied the top to bring it home to her.

That kind of dream recurred when I saw her fish and catch nothing.
Why should she struggle with that, I thought. The river's gaping mouth
Begs for a weir with an opening halfway. I'll paddle out,
Crying "The ocean is running out of water, Fish, you'll die.
This is the end of the world unless you follow me through here."
Mackerel, pollock, cod, herring, sturgeon – every fish came in,
Wanting my river: so full that when I shut the weir, I saw
Some of them pushing each other out and flapping on the shore.
"Reach in and grab what you like," I thought, but each time waking up,
Back with her and where we lived, I felt the ocean and the light
Parting my lips. "Let them go." Instead of all of them dying,
What would the dream of a new sun and a new ocean reveal?
More than the cracks inside granite scraped by glaciers on the coast,
Each of them like an evolving story, no original
Other than making the version different from the one before?
Whether it actually happened or remained a state of mind,
Meant for a chosen few or the many if they wanted it,
Could be important but not as much as what could have been missed,
Even though being there, fiction or not, long ago or now.
Seeing this made me a poet, and still, they remember me.

Animals teach people
Fight continuously
They remember me
I prey not preyed upon

And have a plan to stay
By catching everything
To save them in the end
So they remember me

I save them for my love
But she says, let them go
Like ocean, light, and land
And they remember me

Who made the wind such a struggle? Why would I walk into it,
Sure, I'd find out when the only choice was stop or turn around?
Not that I had a choice but the will to know and keep going.
Wind in the waves, in the valleys, in the hills, through the mountains;
Wind through the trees and then all the trees blown down; wind in my face,
Harder and harder until it seemed to take my face with it.
Blank I felt even my body had been taken. I was air,
And I heard, "I'm the first. My wings move first. Then you'll find your voice,
Only when I want." The wind stopped, and I thought "Did I do that?"
Two-sided anti-gusts of elation and abandonment
Filled in the absolute stillness, and I left there overcome.
Never had I felt so calm. The tree line parted, and the hills
Seemed to slope down in love with the glassed off ocean stretching out
Like it would never stop other than to free a gorgeous wave.
Finally, no wind and no struggle. I would stay there all my life –
Stagnating water, the brown scum thick to move in, and the fish
Floating dead or slowly surfacing their empty gills for air
Massively bug swarmed, where I gasped, too, and hopelessly sweaty:
Part of pollution – how not to be – but once more I would hear,
"My wings first. I'm the first. You'll find your voice only when I want."

Bright wings
And the wind of winds
Blow me away

My voice
And the calm of creation
Die in a day

Bright wings
And the wind of winds
Come my way

Some words
In the wings of creation
I can say

Going against the wind, what would I become without its voice?
Voice or not what about when I had to fight the cold alone?
Stopping or turning away from it come at me all around?
No more corn growing, the flowers going gray to brown to gone,
Emptiness echoing flatly leafless trees to wasting fields,
Hunger, and hiding, unless I found the one fire warm enough,
Like I was really a species living way above the snow
Burying tops of the evergreens locked deeply in the ice.
Add darkness longer and longer making all the white on white
Seizing the chance to shine preternaturally bright, as if
Frozen in deep blue eyes, how could simple feelings like "I'm cold...
I'm almost frozen...I'm frozen to death" over and over,
Lost in such beauty not seem like dreaming and not waking up?
Yet when I did in the dusk, unsure if merely afternoon
Or many months had passed since I'd slept so deeply, I could hear

Only the wail and the wide and slow vibrato of a loon.
Also, a warm breeze first touched my arm and kissed me on the mouth.
Getting up, walking south I first saw her. "Sail away with me.
You're all I've wanted and needed." Stepping lightly in her boat,
I saw the dorsal fin of a sail, jumped out, and pushed her off.

> *Coldest cold, darkest dark*
> *Mind of nothing, white on white*
> *Buried trees I dwell above*
> *And freeze to death, alone in love*

> *How long, who knows, asleep, a dream,*
> *A keening loon, the first warm breeze*
> *Touches my arm, opens my mouth,*
> *I'll be more careful walking south*

As I walked more, passing lots of people, some obsessed with cold,
Others with being warm, strangely none of them seemed to see me.
"Wings of the spring, earth's beginning," I sang. Could no one hear me?
Finally, one person did, and she talked to me. So, when I said,
"I'm cold...I'm frozen to death," it seemed like I had said nothing.
As for the dead corn, the voided flowers, the trees stripped to their bones,
Endlessly echoing empty driven into real hunger
And into hiding without a fire to stop the ice and snow
Burying body and soul with no escape in the darkness:
Tell me, she said, what about them, and I felt myself melting.
Cawing and kraaing chopped into rattles, clicks and distant bells,
As if the crows said, don't talk, keep moving toward her. And I did,
Like the snow melting and running down a river with dead leaves.
Looking back, I saw my footprints getting greener and greener.
Only it wasn't me getting closer. She had come to me:
Putting the lilacs in my arms and the lupines at my knees;

Opening irises in my eyes and poppies for my dreams.
Robin and cardinal, goldfinch, chickadee, and song sparrow.
What did I think: I had made them or that I'd keep them away?
No matter how cold, she'd be there, just like I'd be there for her.

Only she knows that I'm here
Singing my joy and my fear
Somewhere between hot and cold
Unseen, unheard in the crowd

Not that she answers out loud
As I get closer and see
She's the one moving not me
And that I've fallen in grass

Lupines and lilacs en masse,
Irises, poppies, with birds
Lifting our hearts in the air,
Still, we could be anywhere

Unknown to most we lived blithely in our out of the way place:
Next to a stream with great water but the only one around.
Nutime explored it, and I became intent to find the spring
Or if a bunch of springs pooled came down the mountains to the bay.
Meanwhile, I saw the stream run low and not only in summer.
Even in autumn, the dry land knew enough to form puddles
With all the rain, but the stream could only sink into its bed,
Taking my spirits down with it. Better get used to being
Dry as a bone in the ashes of a fire. Winter, snow, ice,
And Nutime melting: all failed to stop the water running out.
Turtles and fish dried out on the cracked clay banks of my dead stream:
Dead as the trees it deserted after stripping off their shade;

Empty as cries of the babies with no hope of getting fed.
"Pitiful," I would say, "pitiful," when my loons looked to me,
As if a trickle of muddy water thought up in my head
Might send them off when I really felt like singing to the skies,
"Do what you like, and I won't care. Go get water someplace else."
There I sat swollen with all my thirst become self-importance:
Big yellow eyes stuck out from my head like pine-knots to be poked;
Mouth a straight-line ear to ear, my toes and fingers' long gnarled roots.

Nutime heard "Water no water" in the loon wail tremolos.
Sending the messenger wolves and thinking how they thrived on thirst
Might be endearing, but their wails down to whimpers – "You get none.
"You get none" – and their eyes blinking me beyond recognition,
When they returned had to be surprising, or so I would think.
But she stayed calm, reassuring and said, "So, I'll go myself."
Only she looked very different now, as I would soon find out:
Twice as tall, head shaven with a tuft of hair left on the top
Wrapped in a hundred long feathers, alternating red and black;
Also, her face painted like fresh blood and green rings round her eyes;
Large clam shell earrings, and on her back a bald-headed eagle
Flapping its wings spread out wide. That's how she came to me and said,
"Clooscape, I want your best water. You must give it to me now."
Spitting, I wanted to scream, "You're crazy. No! The water's gone,"
Only it wasn't, I couldn't talk, my mouth became too dry,
Feeling the torrent and waves of water bursting out of me
Where the flint blade in her hand kept plunging, plunging, and plunging.
Was I a leech in wet, cool mud, or a frog jumping on rocks?
Maybe a crab on the tides? A fish in water constantly?
"Get me some water, please," Nutime said. So, I got up and did,

Stream of great water	*Only one around*
Streams us together	*From unknown sources*
Only I see it	*Running low and dry*
Where I must follow	*Where she also dies*
Loons crying, hear me	*Wolves singing, listen*
I have no pity	*Get your own water*
Water no water	*And you'll get no more*
Enter warrior	*Give me the water*
Your best water now	*No! The water's gone*
She rips me open	*And we almost drown*
We sleep together	*She wakes up thirsty*
Asks for some water	*I get up for her*

Over my no-water paranoia when she needed me:
Simply her asking for water when we really had plenty.
Cattails along the stream often whispered why I was afraid:
Back to my childhood, my brother, how I had to survive him.
Living a lot in the water, like I was amphibian:

Hefty, sleek, dark pelted swimmer's body down to my one big
Powerful fantasized rudder as I flared my incisors
Longer and longer – not that this stopped his coming after me.
Like he came first in the world and, therefore, had sole dominion.
Only he didn't, though in my innocence and adapting
I thought he'd change as I tried to build my own little kingdom:
Laying out ponds among dams that anyone could call their own;
White birches marking the boundaries of the meadows round my streams.
Simply to hear them play by themselves like magic tambourines
Set me in motion, though more at night when he couldn't see me.
Nor would he ever come close to dreaming blossoms and fresh air
Could be enough, trailing lace of cedar smoke and vanilla
Like whom I followed once, deep down through a small hole in the ice
As if she could have been Nutime, sparing me from what I faced:
Fresh water would be forbidden, and whenever I got close

Boulders and vast chunks of earth he'd hurl at me and that would miss
Landed like islands of hate and like they'd never wear away.
Why should what I made or liked not be what he wanted to break,
Pulverized into the sand for the next tide to sweep to sea?
So, we went back and forth. Neither stronger than his twin brother.
Hearing him claim he'd kill all my children and stretch out their skins
Far as the eye could see, and that someday I should thank him, too,
What should I do, bite his balls off or bend down and bite off mine,
Throwing them at him and walk away like I conquered the world?
Faster in water or eating all the trees didn't matter.
Nor would committing a fratricide with feathers or cattails.
So, he came after me like a beaver deep in the river.
Thrashing each other down to the bottom would come to nothing.
As would his changing himself into a snake, since I did, too,
Or more unnamable monsters, since our struggling only churned
More and more mud in the water so that who won the battle

Couldn't be seen, and it seemed the fighting still was going on.
"Get me a little more water, please," I heard my Nutime call.
Wading back from where I'd wandered by myself in the cattails,
And as I handed her the container, she said, "Where were you?"

> *Back in the cattails you find me*
> *Escaping all my cares*
> *Lost in memory*

> *No immortality*
> *War everywhere*
> *Back in the cattails you find me*

> *Living marginally*
> *In the water and the air*
> *Lost in memory*

> *First place I ever felt free*
> *With nothing to bear*
> *Back in the cattails you find me*

> *Unless she*
> *Calls, I'm unaware*
> *Lost in memory*

> *If anybody wants my story*
> *Like how I killed my brother there*
> *Back in the cattails you find me*
> *Lost in memory*

E.6

Where was I? Where would I be without her and our child, Quoddy?
Off on some island left by myself with no way to get back:
Not until I became lower than the animals and birds,
Yet without finding a single egg. Behold, the great hunter,
Ignorant in isolation, thinking I'd make wilderness
Into my fasting with prayers and dreams for more strength and power,
As if my insensate anger wouldn't cut me off from force.
I didn't even know how to swim, deluded by a fox
Waving its tail to grab onto or to drown far off from shore.
Or when that failed, I imagined being saved by a huge whale,
Putting me on its back, as if I already hadn't heard
Clams singing in shallow water, "We'll throw you in the ocean."
Life without Nutime and Quoddy: I remember where I was;
Eating my own lice as if my teeth were cracking cranberries;
Sharpening both of my elbows so that no one could get close.
Yet who would want to? I'd driven that thought furthest from my mind:
Looking for water to muddy and pollute with my bad sense;
Sweating in layers of magic bear meat wrapped around my neck.
Letting my dogs loose and saying "stop," but knowing they'd attack.
I'd be a witch, male and female, making war upon myself,

Like someone whom I once loved but who refused my affections;
Like someone older who ruled my life, and whom I'd overthrown,
Punishing him all my life and making sure I took his place.
Life without Nutime and Quoddy – I would wander off from them.
Hadn't I choked that wolf with a bunch of cattails in the marsh,
Long ago leaving him dead? I clearly wanted to be him
Back alive, the only one important – seeing no one else.
Finding the narrowest pass among the mountains to get through,
Loaded down with all my weapons; then with nothing in my way,
Building the hemlock bark, final fire with what I thought I knew;
Me jumping in with "I love you, love you," turning into ash.

Yet as a wolf walking – head down and my nose close to the ground –
I'd leave this fire behind, planning to compose it as a song.
Not that my singing, self-immolating, and then surviving
Let me feel less hurt and less pain from the act of existing.
Stung by this minute by minute, day by day, and year by year
Had to be how to live or I would become delusional.
Knowing the truth, how could I not make it sing to everyone.
Trying, I merely buzzed, back in bed with Nutime, and she groaned,
"Please, Clooscape, kill that mosquito, since it keeps waking me up."

> *I am the witch of low, senseless, cheating, empty self-denial*
> *Fleeing, repulsive, deluded, sweaty, greasy, and hostile*
> *Neuter, amoral, infested, hurting, burned, armed, fake, and tricked*
> *Lost, alone, drowned, stung, polluting, felon, reject, parched, adrift*
> *I am the witch of my own war and self-making in my head*
> *Buzz in her ear when I'm dreaming, cozy, next to her in bed*

After a few seconds and remembering my awful dream,
What a relief to know I was in my bed and next to her,
Even though she woke me up and rolling over back to sleep,
Blankets pulled up to her head, so that I woke up three more times
Slapping the buzz in my ears before I finally killed the witch,
No, the mosquito. I didn't have to think long where I'd be
If Nutime hadn't come with me but stayed with her family.
But if I didn't take care of her while she took care of me,
What if she went back, a long-lost child, and she took Quoddy, too?
Of if we both stayed when we were young. I had no family.
If I adopted her father and her mother as my own;
Same with her brothers and sisters: we would also be siblings.
Could I be one of them? What if they turned out to be evil?
Nutime and Quoddy weren't with me when I went back to find out,
Down to the family homestead in the Saco River sands.

One-eyed and old, half gray like a stony mountain, the father
Sat in his house, and I walked in, looking exactly like him.
Passing nearby, his sons heard us talking and they peaked inside.
No hair of difference between us scared them, and they cried, "He's here,"
Knowing I came back with power and could do away with them.

Seeing us eating a whale's tail on a birchbark newly peeled,
One brother grabbed it from me and said, "Our meat's too good for you."
"That's for me," I calmly said, and it flew back into my hands.
This made the brothers walk out, but one said, "Maybe it's not him."
Soon they returned, and the oldest held a whale jawbone. "Watch this."
Bending it with all his might, he smiled. "I hope I don't scare you.

Give it a try," he said, handing this huge, heavy thing to me.
No one expected I'd take it in one hand between my thumb
And index finger and snap it like a twig, but when I did,
I heard the youngest say, "I heard that he died. Let's smoke with him."
So, they brought in a huge pipe and filled it up to pass around.
When it came last to me, dumping out the ash I filled the bowl
Full as could be until all the smoke was in me and I laughed.
"Let's play a ball game," the older brother said, and threw a skull
Snapping its teeth at me, which I caught and threw into the sand.
Water burst out of it, forming a gigantic wave I rode,
Seeing the brothers dragged out to sea and changed into sturgeon,
Barbels for wampum around their necks without humanity.
Yet I heard Nutime say, "Clooscape. Sorry, I woke you last night.
Time to get up and make breakfast. Let's have caviar and eggs."

> *Mother died giving us birth*
> *Brother died at my own hands*
> *And I'm lost dreaming alone*
>
> *Or I'm surrounded by hate*
> *History wanting me dead*
> *And I will never create*
> *Family I call my own*
>
> *I'll have my stories instead*
> *Is that how much they are worth?*
> *Waking up, I understand*

Watching her fingers stroke up and down and press the white belly
Of her pet sturgeon induced to labor spewing golden eggs
Brought back the hunger when I first said, "My life is in your hands,"
Echoing "My life in your hands" and creation in her voice.

How were we saved and not overcome until oblivion?
Simply to wonder this back then made me feel invincible,
Thinking I knew all about what I had never experienced:
Much less that I would be overwhelmed by it to live in peace.
Hunting down all of the animals to save them in the end,
Making sure my net caught every fish for me to let them go,
Tracking the whirlwinds to stillness where I had to find my voice
Freezing itself to death in the hope that I would be like Spring –
Then meeting Nutime; not even when I murdered my brother
And being born on a beach had power like our baby's birth:
Power I couldn't imagine; power I couldn't handle:
Real, that is, unlike the stories in my head that I made up;
Stories become the tradition, legends, folk tales, fables, myths
All about me as a hero of the Dawnland and the world,
Yet to be true to my name, my fiction, and my poetry.
I was a man with a wife and child, and we lived near a stream.

Nutime said, "Clooscape, you're lucky. He just woke up from his nap.
Otherwise, you'd have to wait to see him. Babies like to sleep.
And please remember, no maple sugar candy. He could choke."
Seeing our baby crawl on the bearskin blanket made me smile.
"Come here," I said, and he also smiled at me but didn't budge.
Hearing him giggle or more like gurgle, when I made the sound
Didn't affect him, so I tried singing like a little bird.
"Quoddy boy, Quoddy boy, come to Daddy," I called him again.
Down on his belly he turned away as if I disappeared.
Not giving up, automatically I lapsed into the voice
That I heard telling the stories in my head and that I used
Telling them so that they sounded true no matter what I said –
No matter how strange or supernatural they made me seem.
As if he liked it, his stare grew bright, but he came no closer.
Even though I had prevailed in them, it didn't help me here.

Tossing his little toy of some deerskin sewn like a turtle
Up in the air, I said, "Stay there. Don't move. I don't really care,"
Under my breath, and he started crying louder and louder.
When I yelled just as loud, "Nutime," she came back and picked him up,
Lifting her shirt to give him the breast, and both of us calmed down.

Her hand, my life, her life, my hand
Imagine, much less understand
By one our being less alone
Otherwise, the same unknown

The made-up, and quotidian,
Except we're less alone again
Having a baby, so I attest
And sing the power of the breast

Mother a turtle. Twin brother of a wolf. Behold the man
Not knowing what I was born to do but lost in wishes like
I'd be alluring, looked up to, strong, resilient, and rooted;
Fine for a pine tree or cedar, but so many get cut down.
Wishes the long-ago sound that played to make people happy,
Lost since I saw so much sadness, could be more than a screech owl
Answering cries for attention dying in their own echoes;
Wishes for love as if hunting could feed everyone hungry;
Wishes like muscles I stripped off some dead whale for my body.
Wishes like white doves becoming women wild all over me:
Teeming and glowing with long arms, open legs, and bared chests pushed
Into my face kissing all I could until I had no more.

Nor did they quit on me, leaving only body parts and bones
After the swarm vanished into no one, nowhere, and nothing.
Wishes becoming my stories not attributed to me:
Changed into powers I granted as the wishes of others:
Happiness, riches, love, cunning, looks, strength, cure-alls, and no death–
As if I wasn't like everyone who wanted the same things:
As if I no more could have them for myself except as dreams:
Stories sung back to me as the hero I knew I wasn't.

Nor did I need to be whether I lived thirteen thousand-years
In the same place or not: speaking the same languages or not;
Six thousand, four thousand, two or one, I knew I'd seen enough,
Living with Nutime and Quoddy and secure beside the stream.
"Clooscape," I heard her say, "Look who's sleeping now. Get up and shave
Your ancient rock of a face. Where are you under all that moss?"
Had I been sleeping? I wondered. She was just nursing Quoddy.
She looked a hundred years old now, feeble, bent, and decrepit.
Quoddy came in and said smiling, "Mother. I've brought four beavers.
We won't be hungry." But I saw Nutime barely could lift them.
"Quoddy, you make them," I said, "Your mother wants to wash her face."
Yet I went with her to watch what happened all the times before.
Water washed over her leaving her face smooth and very clear.
Young again, she combed her hair no longer gray but shining dark.
Straight and full, she wore a soft, thin robe and walked into my arms.
Tall trees with gardens among them burgeoned down into the sea.
How it created the light around our land and purest air
Dazed us as always, as if we had forgotten it before.
"Clooscape enough," Nutime whispered to me, looking in the mirror.
"Now that you've cleaned yourself up, you're ready. Come to bed, my man."

What is my legacy? See
What is my belief? A leaf
What does the owl screech? Reach
And when I hunt and shoot? Hoot
A dead whale makes me strong. Wrong
What if I go on the make? Ache
I want to stake my claim. Lame
What if my dreams are the hero? Oh
Would anybody care? Air
But if they were true? You
And the unpredictable? Bull
What should I reply? Lie
The dreams keep rising. Sing
Whether fiction or fact. Act
Changing they replay. Play
Whose dreams aren't epic? Pick

People and animals used to speak one language but not now.
They were all different. I called them. No one answered anymore,
And I had nothing to say, as if our feasting together
Time after time at the silver water's edge never happened.
No one would care, much less come if I invited them again.
Thinking we learned from each other simply how to be happy,
Open, and grateful succumbed to fear of death we were born with,
Pushing me to a point where I didn't know my directions:
Far out to sea and beyond the other side of any clouds;
Into the west or the dawn, I couldn't tell my north or south
Coming or going, except I knew I had to get away.
So said my wolves changed to graveyard islands waiting for a storm;
So said my loons cutting all their notes to one and sounding sad:
So said the white snowy owl's seeming vow to disappear
Into the darkest, deep forest with no more than "I'm sorry."

So said the towering purple basalt cliff right in my face,
If I could see it for once and not drift into silly dreams.
What did I think I was doing when I made all those arrows,
As if it passed the time in the same way Nutime's making food
Merely prepared us for how we lived together day to day.

Hearing the rumble and seeing loosened boulders tumble down
Into the surge of a storm tide like there was no tomorrow
Even the greenest and tallest pine trees never would survive,
Much less the leaves trembling off the branches as my warning sign,
Now was the time, and I knew that finally the great war had come.
Fighting it I could save no one, nothing. All of humankind,
Animals, earth, and sky – this war no life ever could endure.
Still, I had no idea when the battle might come to an end:
Maybe a day or so, or a hundred years – maybe longer.
As for the prophecy my descendants would remember me?
What was I thinking? That we weren't always hunting in darkness?
Or if we died that there'd be a way for someone to pull us
Out of the burial mounds or tree trunks where we tried to hide?
"I'll birth myself" was the answer. My twin brother, Malsum's voice
Back from the womb where I asked him how he wanted to be born
Screamed as we struggled to kill each other deep in the cattails.
Spitting out feathers, I heard him growling over and over,
"How do you want to die, Clooscape. Tell me how you want to die."
I could be dreaming or dying, but I couldn't stop singing,
"Kill me. You won't kill my stories. I am Clooscape the poet."

> *I don't want to think about the future*
> *Tomorrow's crumbling basalt in my face*
> *A constant war and nature in a rage*
> *All language prey to fear of death again*
> *Provisions merely adding to the waste*

The brute exposure, loss of all direction
No trees survive and no one can remember
Owls vowing no escape and no return
My wolves like barren islands for my loons
Reduced to one last cry how they forsake
A man, a wife, a child without a cure
I don't want to think about my brother
Killing my mother and trying to kill me
Like I'm no more than stories and my name

But then another voice joined mine, Nutime's, saying something else.
 "Clooscape. It's usually me who falls asleep, but not this time.
Both of us did, and I'll get up first. I'm hungry. You stay here.
Quoddy by now has the steaks cut, and I'll start making dinner."
Then she left, trailing the covers, which I pulled back on the bed.
Where would we be if we listened to the shaman years ago?
Why did I think he had visions, power, and desire to say
That we had met like the seasons coming out of each other?
Why did our sexual being throw him off, though we agreed
Ever since that he was right, ironically, as we laughed;
Only wrong thinking it wouldn't last and wasn't a reason
For me to leave behind making rules for what he created:
Everything changing shape, no exceptions – not even persons.
Or I was given the power to transform them into stone
Perfectly shaped like a moose, a pretty little bird, my dogs,
Bones and the head of some fish I ate, or like an old woman,
Rather than being the stories I made up about myself:
Lies with some wisdom: respected, true, and not always believed.
Why did the shaman see nothing but red-ant-infested log
Where I found freedom and love to live before and after death?

Look at that white deerskin ermine-tail-trimmed robe with the bear teeth
Hung in the corner beside the wren-skin shawl reminding me
How we shot maple wood bows strung tight with cattails, and we aimed
Arrows to find our new home by running to the place they fell,
Where we would shoot them and run but faster, faster, and faster,
Almost forgetting our bodies to be one with the arrows,
So that we finally were catching them ourselves before landing;
So that we knew the path that we followed had to be our own.
Nutime would die in a famine. I'd be buried in the waves.
How could the plants and the animals survive our stream gone dry?
Climbing the mountains around us up and down to find its source
Previous times I had failed, but now I had to try again.
Nutime and Quoddy stayed home and hoped a mostly mud trickle,
Dead leaves, and me somehow coming back with water were enough.
This time I wouldn't give up. I'd find it. And I would be back,
Gourds full of water, but where were Nutime, Quoddy, and our home?

Flat, clear-cut, empty space and a filled-up hole sealed with a stone
Blood red with sacrifice spoke the words: return of the shaman.
Shreds of white deerskin and sewn wren feathers, tufts of ermine fur:
Now I remembered the vision that the shaman dreamed for me.

> *Husband and wife at home with their child and happy –*
> *What about being warned that they never could be?*
> *New lives and joys they find living by their stream*
> *Really are shadows of death and their false dream*
> *Never fulfilled and forgotten – if not forsaken...*
> *Or it's the everyday with a story to awaken*

Nutime would offer herself as sacrifice to the end the drought,
And I'd obey her no matter how much we cried together,
Listening to what the shaman told us like he was a god,
Knowing how we could be saved, and I could keep our world alive.
Sparks in her raven hair, face like snow, her blood red cheeks, her robe
Slipping and radiant from her body coming like a storm –
How could I do it until she grabbed my arm, stone axe in hand,
Yanking it full strength so deep inside her throat I couldn't see
Through all the blood what had happened, as the shaman predicted
When I first told him I couldn't do it. "God will give you strength
At the right moment, so you'll see and feel nothing, as you won't
Dragging her by the hair seven times and seven times seven
Yet seven more up and down the fields you once had called your home:
So that her bones stripped of every bit of flesh can be buried
After you've dug a hole in the middle, sealed with this red stone,"
Which he pressed into my hands and took back like he was unsure.
As well he should have been. We weren't listening to what he said.
All those years later when drought and famine hit, I only did
What any man would do, finding water for my family.
This let the shaman return and get his way once and for all.

Wasn't I waking up? Where was Malsum? Had I died three times?
Killing him, freezing to death in love with cold, and Nutime gone;
Lost in the shaman's unknowing and forgetting her power?
There I was sailing alone, my pockets filled with broken gourds.
Both shores of Passamaquoddy Bay closed in, becoming cliffs.
Barely myself rode the steep, strong tide king high and still coming...
When the first breached in my eyes: the stocky black and vast smooth back;
But then another, another, and a lot of different kinds:
V-shaped and streamlined; or huge rectangle skulls with ancient eyes;
Dorsal fins coming in gray, brown, black, and white yet all at once:
Hooked into sickles or killer straight up, which scared me the most.
Whale after whale after whale ploughed up the bay, and I watched them:
One by one and then together breaching. Two of the biggest
Mid-air collided, and more whales started crashing each other:
Up and down, back and forth, sideways pounding into the battle
Thrashing the whole bay to white before it changed to bloody brown
After the fighting went nowhere, and I couldn't change my course:
Sailing right into my stories, Clooscape, Clooscape the poet.
No one might hear me but Nutime, and I heard her calling me.
"Clooscape. We're waiting. Where are you? Clooscape. Clooscape the poet!"

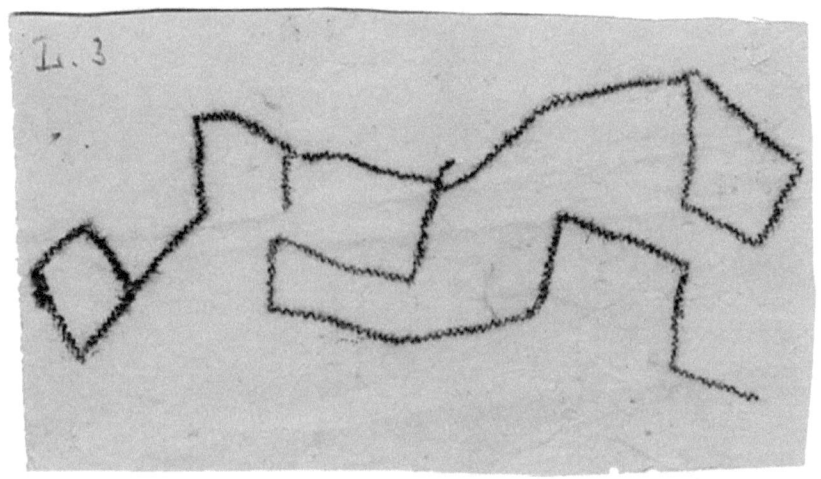

BIBLIOGRAPHY

Adney, Edwin Tappen. *Edwin Tappan Adney Papers.* Philips Library, Peabody Essex Museum. https://pem.as.atlas-sys.com/repositories/2/resources/489.

Alger, Abby Langdon. *In Indian Tents: Stories Told by Penobscot, Passamaquoddy and Micmac Indians to Abby L. Alger.* Roberts Brothers, 1897.

Augustine, Stephen. "The Mi'kmaq Creation Story." Nova Scotia Curriculum. https://curriculum.novascotia.ca/sites/default/files/documents/resource-files/Mi_kmaq%20Creation%20Story%20%28as%20told%20by%20Stephen%20Augustine%29.pdf.
----- *Mi'kmaq & Maliseet Cultural Ancestral Material.* Canadian Museum of Civilization Corporation, 2005.
----- *Extended Creation Story.* Unama'ki College. https://www.youtube.com/watch?v=rZdV39J5j7s.

Bangor Daily News. "Wayne A Newell (April 16, 1942 – December 23, 2021)." https://obituaries.bangordailynews.com/obituary/wayne-newell-1084081092.

Barratt, Joseph, and Nicola Tenesles. *The Indian of New-England, and the North-Eastern Provinces: A Sketch of the Life of an Indian Hunter, Ancient Traditions Relating to the Etchemin Tribe, Their Modes of Life, Hunting, &c.: With Vocabularies in the Indian and English, Giving the Names of the Animals, Birds, and Fish, the Most Complete That Has Been Given for New-England in the Languages of Etchemin and Micmacs.* Charles H. Pelton, 1851. DigitalCommons@UMaine, https://digitalcommons.library.umaine.edu/cgi/viewcontent.cgi?article=1276&context=maine-history.

Beck, Horace P. *Gluskap the Liar and Other Indian Tales*. B. Wheelwright Company, 1966.

Bourque, Bruce J. *Twelve Thousand Years: American Indians in Maine*. With contributions by Steven L. Cox and Ruth H. Whitehead. University of Nebraska Press, 2001.

Brinton, Daniel G. "The Hero-God of the Algonkins as a Cheat and Liar." *Essays of an Americanist*. Porter & Coates, 1890. https://www.gutenberg.org/ebooks/58464.

Brooks, Lisa Tanya. *The Common Pot: The Recovery of Native Space in the Northeast*. University of Minnesota Press, 2008.
----- *Our Beloved Kin: A New History of King Philip's War*. Yale University Press, 2018.

Brooks, Lisa and Kelly Wisecup (eds.). *Plymouth Colony: Narratives of English Settlement and Native Resistance from the Mayflower to King Philip's War*. Library of America, 2022.

Bruchac, Joseph. *The Wind Eagle and Other Abenaki Stories*. Bowman Books 1985.
----- *The Faith Hunter, Abenaki Stories*. Greenfield Review Press, 1988.
----- *Return of the Sun: Native American Tales from the Northeast Woodlands*. Crossing Press, 1989.
----- *Roots of Survival: Native American Storytelling and the Sacred*. Fulcrum Press, 1996.

Bryant, Rachel. "The Last of the Wabanakis: Absolution Writing in Atlantic Canada." *Settler Colonial Studies* 10, no. 1 (2020):1-14.

Campbell, Joseph. *Historical Atlas of World Mythology*. Perennial Library, 1988.

Chamberlain, A. F. "The Thunder-Bird Amongst the Algonkins." *American Anthropologist* 3, no. 1 (1890): 51-54.

Confederacy of Mainland Mi'kmaq. *Kekina'muek: Learning about the Mi'kmaq of Nova Scotia*. Eastern Woodland Publishing, 2007.

Dana, Carol. *When No One is Looking*. Lulu.com, 2011.
----- *Return to Spirit and Other Musings*. Lulu.com, 2014.

Dana, Carol, Margo Lukens, and Conor M. Quinn, *"Still They Remember Me": Penobscot Transformer Tales*. University of Massachusetts Press, 2021.

Day, Gordon M. *In Search of New England's Native Past*. Michael K. Foster and William Cowan (eds.). University of Massachusetts Press, 1998.

DeBlois, Albert D. *Micmac Texts*. Canadian Museum of Civilization, 1990.

Downeast Fisheries Trail and Roosevelt-Campobello International Park, "Passamaquoddy People / Les Passamaquoddys / Peskotomuhkatiyik." *Maine Sea Grant Publications* 35 (2014).

Dozay, Arlene Christmas. *Kluskap of the Wabanaki*. Abbe Museum and National Park Service, 2015.

Eastport, ME. "Eastport Maine Comprehensive Plan" (2018). *Maine Town Documents*. 6817.

Eckstorm, Fannie Hardy. "Maine Indian Legends 1917" (2018). *Fannie Hardy Eckstorm Papers.* Submission 34. https://digitalcommons.library.umaine.edu/eckstorm_papers/34.

----- "Maine Indian Legends – undated" (2018). *Fannie Hardy Eckstorm Papers.* Submission 40. https://digitalcommons.library.umaine.edu/eckstorm_papers/40.

Elder, William. "The Aborigines of Nova Scotia." *North American Review* 112, no. 230 (1871): 1-30.

Fauset, Arthur Huff. "Folklore from the Half-Breeds in Nova Scotia." *The Journal of American Folklore* 38, no. 148 (1925): 300-15.

Francis, David A., Robert M Leavitt, and Margaret Apt. *Peskotomuhkati Wolastoqewi Latuwewakon: A Passamaquoddy-Maliseet Dictionary.* University of Maine Press; Fredericton, Goose Lane Editions, 2008. Cf. Passamaquoddy-Maliseet Language Portal. https://pmportal.org.

Francis, Michael. *The Micmac Legend of our Seasons.* Micmac Indian Craftsmen, 1963
----- *The Micmac Legend of the Wild Goose.* Micmac Indian Craftsmen, 1963.
----- *The Legend of the Tidal Bore.* Micmac Indian Craftsmen, 1963.
----- *The Mimac Legend of Tatler, the Loon* (1964). New Brunswick Museum, New Brunswick Craft Collection, 1995.
----- *The Mimac Legend of Talker, the Owl* (1964). New Brunswick Museum, New Brunswick Craft Collection, 1995.

Fewkes, J. Walter. "A Contribution to Passamaquoddy Folklore." *Journal of American Folk-Lore* III, no, XI (1890): 259-80. https://digitalcommons.library.umaine.edu/cgi/viewcontent.cgi?article=1509&context=mainehistory.

Gordon, Arthur Hamilton. *Wilderness Journeys in New Brunswick 1862-63*. J.& A. M'Millan Publishers, 1864.

Gregory, Alice. "How Did a Self-Taught Linguist Come to Own an Indigenous Language." *The New Yorker* (April 12, 2021).

Hager, Stansbury. "Micmac Customs and Traditions." *American Anthropologist* 8, no. 1 (1895): 31-42.
----- "Weather and the Seasons in Micmac Mythology." *The Journal of American Folklore* 10, no. 37 (1897):101-05.

Hassencahl-Perley, Emma, and John Leroux. *Wabanaki Modern, Wabaaki Kiskukewey, Wabanaki Moderne*. Goose Lane Editions, 2022.

Hatcher, Annamarie. "My Past is my Present in my Future: Indigenous Ways of Knowing and the Climate Change Discourses." *Climate Change Across the Curriculum*. Eric J. Fretz (ed.). Lexington Books, 2016, 167-82.

Higashikawa, Yoichi. "A Note on the Kluskap Story-Cycle: An Introduction to Micmac Story." *Hakodate Eibungaku: Journal of the English Literary Society of Hakodate* 32 (March 31, 1993): 1–12.

Higashikawa, Yoichi, and Masatsuga Kimura. "Kluskap and Mi'kmaq Spiritualism." *Hakodate Eibungaku: Journal of the English Literary Society of Hakodate* 32 (March 31, 1993): 13–22.

Hill, Kay. *Glooscap and His Magic*. McClelland and Stewart, 1963.
----- *More Glooscap Stories: Legends of the Wabanaki Indians*. McClelland and Stewart, 1970.

Holyoke, Kenneth R, and M. Gabriel Hrynick (eds.). *The Far Northeast: 3000 BP to Contact.* University of Ottawa Press, 2022.

Hornborg, Alf. "Environmentalism, Ethnicity, and Sacred Places: Reflections on Modernity, Discourse, and Power." *Canadian Review of Sociology and Anthropology* 31, no. 3 (1994): 245–67.

Hornborg, Anne-Christine. "Kluskap as Culture Hero and Global Green Warrior: Different Context for the Canadian Culture Hero." *Acta Americana,* 9, no. 1 (2001): 17–38.
----- "A Landscape of Left-Overs: Changing Conceptions of Place and Environment Among Mi'Kmaq Indians of Eastern Canada." *Lund Studies in History of Religions,* 14. Religionshistoriska avdelningen, Lunds Universiteit, 2001.
----- *Mi'kmaq Landscapes: From Animism to Sacred Ecology.* Ashgate, 2008.
----- "Readbacks or Tradition? The Kluskap Stories Among Modern Canadian Mi'kmaq." *European Review of North American Studies* 16 (2002): 9–16.
----- "Visiting the Six Worlds: Shamanistic Journeys in Canadian Mi'kmaq Cosmology." *Journal of American Folklore* 119, no. 473 (2006): 312–36.

Hulan, Renée, and Renate Eigenbrod (eds.). *Aboriginal Oral Traditions: Theory, Practice, Ethics.* Fernwood, 2008.

Ives, Edward D. (ed.). "Malecite and Passamaquoddy Tales." *Northeast Folklore* VI. University of Maine, 1964. https://umaine.edu/folklife/publications/northeast-folklore-2/.

Jack, Edward. "Maliseet Legends." *Journal of American Folklore* 8, no. 30 (1895): 193-208.

Joe, Rita. *Song of Ekasoni.* Ragweed Press, 1988.

----- *More Poems of Rita Joe.* Women's Press, 1989.

----- *Song of Rita Joe: Autobiography of a Mi'kmaq Poet.* University of Nebraska Press, 1996.

---- and Leslie Choyce (eds.). *The Mi'kmaq Anthology.* Pottersfield Press, 1977.

----- *We Are the Dreamers: Recent and Early Poetry.* Breton Books, 1999.

Johnson, Frederick. "Notes on Micmac Shamanism." *Primitive Man* 16, nos. 3-4 (1943): 53-80.

Kim, Tammy E. "The Passamaquoddy Reclaim Their Culture through Digital Repatriation." *The New Yorker.* (January 30, 2019).

Kimmerer, Robin Wall. *Braiding Sweetgrass.* Milkweed Editions, 2013.

Knockwood, Stephen. *The True Story of Glooscap.* (Unpublished manuscript), 1969. Mi'kmaq Holdings (V/F V.236 #5), NS ARM Library. https://mikmawarchives.ca/documents/the-true-story-of-glooscap

Kroskrity, Paul V. *Telling Stories in the Face of Danger: Language Renewal in Native American Communities.* University of Oklahoma Press, 2012.

LaCombe, Michele. "More than Where the Heart Is: Meeting Places in Wabanaki Poetry by Cheryl Savageau and Mihku Paul." *Journal of Canadian Studies / Revue d'études canadiennes* 49, no. 2 (2015): 133-49.

Leavitt, Robert M. *Maliseet & Mi'kmaq / First Nations of the Maritimes.* New Ireland Press, 2003.

----- "Storytelling as Language Curriculum." *The Algonquian Papers / Les Actes du Congres des Algonquinistes* 14 (1983): 27-33.

Leavitt, Robert M., and David A. Francis (eds.). *Wapapi Akonutonma-konol, The Wampum Records: Wabanaki Traditional Laws*. University of New Brunswick, 1990.

Lenick, Edward J. "Mythic Creatures: Serpents, Dragons, and Sea Monsters in Northeastern Rock Art." *Archaeology of Eastern North America* 38 (2010): 17-37.

Leland, Charles Godfrey. *Memoirs*, 2 vols. William Heinemann, 1893.
----- "Legends of the Passamaquoddy; With Drawings on Birch Bark by a Quadi Indian." *The Century Illustrated Monthly Magazine* 6 (1884): 668-77.
----- *Algonquin Legends of New England* or *Myths and Folk Lore of the Micmac, Passamaquoddy, and Penobscot Tribes*. Houghton Mifflin and Company,1884.

Leland, Charles Godfrey, and John Dyneley Prince. *Kuloscap the Master, and Other Algonkin Poems*. Funk & Wagnalls Company, 1902.

Lester, Joan A. *History on Birchbark: The Art of Tomah Joseph, Passamaquoddy*. Brown University Press, 1993.

Lesourd, Philip S. "The Passamaquoddy 'Witchcraft Tales' of Newell S. Francis." *Anthropological Linguistics* 42, no. 4 (2000): 441-98.
----- (ed. and trans.). *Tales from Maliseet Country*. University of Nebraska Press 2007.
----- "Four Poems in Passamaquoddy." *Anthropological Linguistics* 60, no. 3 (2018): 195-225.

Lesourd, Philip S., Robert M. Leavitt, and David A. Francis. *Kolusuwakonol: Passamaquoddy-Maliseet & English Dictionary*. Maliseet Institute, 1984.

Lesourd, Philip S., and Conor McDonough Quinn. "How to Swear in Maliseet-Passamaquoddy and Penobscot." *Anthropological Linguistics* 51, no. 1 (2009): 1-37.

Lewis, Roger. Nova Scotia Museum. https://www.facebook.com/profile/100064024059893/search/?q=roger%20lewis.

Long, Charles H. *Alpha: The Myths of Creation.* George Braziller, 1963; Macmillan, 1969; Reprint, Scholars Press, 1983.

Lukens, Margo, and Siobhan Senier. "Introduction." *Indigenous New England: Special Issue on Northeastern Native American Writers. Studies in American Indian Literatures* 24, no. 3 (2012): xi-xviii.

Macmillan, Cyrus. *Glooskap's Country and Other Indian Tales.* Oxford University Press, 1956.

MacDougall, Pauleena. *The Penobscot Dance of Resistance: Tradition in the History of a People.* University of New Hampshire Press, 2004.

Maine Folklife Center, https://umaine.edu/folklife/.

Mallery, Garrick. "The Fight with the Giant Witch." *American Anthropologist* 3, no. 1 (1890): 65-70.

Maillard, L'Abbé (Antoine Simon). *An Account of the Customs and Manners of the Micmakis and Maricheets, Savage Nations, Now Dependent on the Government of Cape-Breton.* S. Hooper and A. Morley, 1758. https://www.gutenberg.org/ebooks/15567.

Mean, Alice, and Arnold Neptune. *Giants of the Dawnland.* Loose Cannon Press, 1996.

McDonald, M. W. "A History of Halifax: A Mi'qmaw Perspective." *Nova Scotia Advocate*. 12 (July 2017). https://nsadvocate.org/wp-content/uploads/2017/07/Halifax-kjipuktuk-history-with-creation-story-1.pdf.

Mechling, W. H. "Malecite Tales." Canada Department of Mines, *Geological Survey* 49, no.4 (1914).

Mehl-Madrona, Lewis. "Gluskabe: A New England Indigenous Cultural Hero Whose Stories Impart Traditional Philosophy." *Etuaptmumk: The Journal of Two-Eyed Seeing* 1, no. 1 (2022): 1-29.

Michelson, Truman. "Micmac Tales." *The Journal of American Folklore* 38, no. 147 (1925): 33-54.

Mitchell, John Bear. "Glooskap, the Great Chief" (2008). https://www.mainememory.net/record/28643.
----- "The Year Summer Was Stolen" (2008). https://www.mainememory.net/record/28644.

Mitchell, Lewis. *Documents Printed by the Order of the Legislature of the State of Maine during the Session A.D. 1887*, no. 251. Burleigh & Flynt, 1888, 1-8.
----- *The Passamaquoddy Wampum Records*. Prince, John Dyneley (ed.). *Proceedings of the American Philosophical Society* 36, no. 156 (1897): 479-95. Cf. *Wapapi Akonutomakonol / The Wampum Records: Wabanaki Traditional Laws*. Francis, Davis A. and Robert Leavitt (eds). Micmac-Maliseet Institute, 1990.
----- "Koluskap at the Annapolis River." (1921). https://plesourd.com/koluskap-at-the-annapolis-river-lewis-mitchell-1921/.

Morningstar Kent, Jeanne. *The Visual Language of Wabanaki* History Press, 2014.

Mundell, Kathleen. *North by Northeast. Wabanaki, Akwesasne Mohawk, and Tuscarora Traditional Arts.* Tilbury House, 2008.

Murphy, Jacqueline Shea. "Replacing Regionalism: Abenaki Tales and Jewett's Coastal Maine." *American Literary History* 10, no. 4 (1998): 664-90.

Newell, Wayne A. (ed.). *Kuhkomossonuk Akonutomuwinokot, Stories Our Grandmothers Told Us.* Resolute Bear Press, 2021.

New York Times. "The Pictured Rocks in Machiasport, ME." October 18, 1869, 2.

Nicolar, J. *The Life and Traditions of the Red Man.* C. H. Glass & Co., 1893.

Nowlan, Alden. *Nine Micmac Legends.* Lancelot Press, 1983.

Ortiz, Simon J. (ed.). *Speaking for the Generations: Native Writers on Writing.* University of Arizona Press, 1997.

Parkhill, Thomas C. *Weaving Ourselves into the Land.* State University of New York Press, 1997.

Parson, Elsie Clews. "Micmac Folklore." *Journal of American Folklore* 38, no. 147 (1925): 55-133.

Paul, Daniel N. *We Were Not the Savages: A Micmac Perspective on the Collision of European and Aboriginal Civilization.* Nimbus, 1993.

Paul, Mihku. *20th Century PowWow Playland.* Bowman Books, 2012.

Paul, William. "Glooscap's Advice." Audio Reel 5048 Recording Number: 195. Shubenacadie, 1944. https://archives.novascotia.ca/mikmaq/exhibit/archives/?ID=128.

----- "Glooscap Predictions." Audio Reel 5096 Recording Number: 680. Shubenacadie, 1944. https://archives.novascotia.ca/creighton/audio/?Search=5096&t=00:16:38.

Partridge, Emelyn Newcomb. *Glooscap the Great Chief and Other Stories*. Sturgis & Walton, 1913.

Passamaquoddy People: At Home on the Ocean and Lakes, https://passamaquoddypeople.com/.

Perry, Margaret. *A Life in Film*. "Glooscap Country." Nova Scotia Information Services, Fc 48, 1958.

Prince, John Dyneley (ed.). "Some Passamaquoddy Witchcraft Tales." *Proceedings of the American Philosophical Society* 38, no. 160 (1899): 181-89.

----- "A Passamaquoddy Tobacco Famine." *International Journal of American Linguistics* 1, no. 1 (1917): 58-63.

Prins, Harald E. *The Mi'kmaq: Resistance, Accommodation, and Cultural Survival*. Wadsworth Publishing, 1996.

Prins, Harald E. L. , and Bunny Mcbride. *Asticou's Island Domain: Wabanaki Peoples at Mount Desert Island 1500-2000*. The Abbe Museum and National Park Service, 2007.

Rand, Silas Tertius. *Legends of the Micmacs*. Longmans, Green and Co., 1894.

Rader, Dean, and Janice Gould (eds.). *Speak to Me Words: Essays on Contemporary American Indian Poetry*. University of Arizona Press, 2003.

Ray, Roger B. "Maine Indians' Concept of Land Tenure." *Maine History* 13, 1 (1973): 29-51.
----- "The Machiasport Petroglyphs." *Maine History* 25, no. 1 (1985): 22-39.
----- "The Embden, Maine, Petroglyphs." *Conservation and Recreation* 27, no. 1 (1987): 14-23.

Reid, Jennifer. *Finding Kluskap: A Journey into Mi'kmaw Myth*. Pennsylvania State University Press, 2013.

Roth, D. Luther. *Acadie and the Acadians*. Lutheran Publication Society, 1890.

Rowe, Paul. S. "Performance vs. Thingification: Linguistic Actions and the Indigenous Literatures of Dawnland Voices." *Literary Matters* (2018), 11.1. https://www.literarymatters.org/11-1-performance-vs-thingification-linguistic-action-and-the-indigenous-literatures-of-dawnland-voices/.

Runningwolf, Michael B., and Patricia Clark Smith. *On the Trail of Elder Brother: Glous'gap Stories of the Micmac Indians*. Persea Books, 2000.

Sappier, Roche. *Glooscap Tales & the Legends of Red E.A.R.T.H.* Red Earth Publishing, 2017.

Savageau, Carol. *Dirt Road Home*. Curbstone Books, 1995.
----- *Out of the Crazywoods*. University of Nebraska Press. 2000.

----- *Voices of American Indian Assimilation and Resistance: Helen Hunt Jackson, Sarah Winnemucca, and Victoria Howard*. University of Oklahoma Press, 2001.

Senier, Siobhan. "'All This / Is Abenaki Country': Cheryl Savageau's Poetic Awikhiganak." *Studies in American Indian Literatures* 22, no. 3 (2010): 1-25.
----- "Rethinking Recognition: Mi'kmaq and Maliseet Poets Re-Write Language and Community." *Melus* 37, no. 1 (2012): 15-34.
----- *Dawnland Voices* (ed.). University of Nebraska Press, 2014.
----- "Bowman Books: A Gathering Place for Indigenous New England." *Studies in American Indian Literatures* 27, no.1 (2015): 96-111.
----- *Sovereignty and Sustainability: Indigenous Stewardship in New England*. University of Nebraska Press, 2020.

Smith, Nicholas N. "Peter Lewis Paul: A Tribute." *Anthropologica* 32, no. 2 (1990): 265-68.

Sockbeson, Rebecca. "Indigenous Research Methodology: Gluskabe's Encounters with Epistemicide." *Postcolonial Directions in Education* 6, no. 1 (2017): 1-27.

Soctomah, Donald. *Passamaquoddy at the Turn of the Century 1890-1920: Tribal Life and Times in Maine and New Brunswick*. Np, 2002.
----- *Hard Times at Passamaquoddy, 1921-1950: Tribal Life and Times in Maine and New Brunswick*. Np, 2003.
----- *Let Me Live as My Ancestors Had 1850-1890: Tribal Life and Times in Maine and New Brunswick*. Np, 2005.
----- *N'tolonapemk: Our Relatives' Place*. With Ellie R. Cowie and Arthur Spiess. Abbe Museum, 2012.
----- *Remember Me: Tomah Joseph's Gift to Franklin Roosevelt*. Tilbury House Publishers, 2015.

Solomon, Viola and Henrietta Black. "Kluskap and His Twin Brother." NA179, T228, 1962. *Northeast Archives of Folklore and Oral History*. Raymond H. Fogler Special Collections Department. University of Maine.

Sotheby. Frank T. The Frank T. Seibert Library of the North American Indian and the American Frontier, vols I & II. Sotheby's, 1999.

Speck, Frank G. "Some Micmac Tales from Cape Breton Island." *The Journal of American Folklore* 28, no. 07, (1915): 59-69.
----- "Malecite Tales." *The Journal of American Folklore* 30, no. 118 (1917): 79-85.
----- "Penobscot Transformer Tales." *International Journal of American Linguistics* 1, no.3 (1918): 187-244.
----- "Penobscot Tales and Religious Beliefs." *The Journal of American Folklore* 48, no. 187 (1937): 1-107.

Spence, Lewis. *The Myths of the North American Indians*. G. G. Harrap, 1914.

Spicer, Stanley. *Glooscap Legends*. Nimbus Publishing, 2006.

Spotted Elk, Molly. *Katahdin: Wigwam Tales of the Abnaki Tribe*. Maine Folklife Center, 2003.

Swann, Brian (ed.). *Voices from Four Directions*. University of Nebraska Press, 2004.
----- *Algonquian Spirit*. University of Nebraska Press, 2005.
----- *Born in the Blood: On Native American Translation*. University of Nebraska Press, 2011.

Swann, Brian and Arnold Krupa(eds.). *Recovering the Word: Essays on Native American Literature*. University of California Press, 1987.

Sweetser, James. *The Maritime Provinces: A Handbook for Travelers*. James R. Osgood & Co., 1875.

Teeter, Karl (ed.). *In Memoriam: Peter Lewis Paul 1902-1989*. University of Ottawa Press, 1993.

Tomah, Dwayne. https://www.youtube.com/watch?v=byrruXgj09U.

Tooker, Willliam Wallace. "Algonquian Names of Some Mountains and Hills." *Journal of American Folklore* 17, no. 66 (1904): 171-79.

Trembley, Tony. *The New Brunswick Encyclopedia (NBLE)*. University of New Brunswick Library, https://nble.lib.unb.ca/new-brunswick-literary-encyclopedia.

Virtual Museum of Canada. *Koluskap: Stories from Wolastoquiyik*. http://website.nbm-mnb.ca/Koluskap/English/index.php.

Wallis, Wilson D. and Ruth Sawtell. *The Micmac Indians of Eastern Canada*. University of Minnesota Press, 1955.

Whitehead, Ruth Holmes. *Stories from the Six Worlds*. Nimbus Publishing Limited, 1988.
----- *Tracking Doctor Lonecloud: Showman to Legend Keeper*. Goose Lane Editions and Nova Scotia Museum, 2002.

Wiseman, Frederick Matthew. *The Voice of the Dawn*. University of New England Press, 2001.

The Wabanakis of Maine and the Maritimes: A Resource book about Penobscot, Passamaquoddy, Maliseet, Micmac and Abenaki Indians, with Lesson Plans for Grades 4 through 8. Prepared and published by The Maine Indian Program of The New England Office of the American Friends Service Committee. Maine Indian Program, 1989.

IMAGES

Cover. "Glooscap Killing His Brother the Wolf." Tomah Joseph. In *Algonquin Legends of New England or Myths and Folk Lore of the Micmac, Passamaquoddy, and Penobscot Tribes.* Charles Godfrey Leland. Boston: Houghton Mifflin and Company,1884. 16. Open access.

Page 12. Tracing of a petroglyph of a hand with cross-hatched palm. George Creed - Petroglyphs Nova Scotia Archives MG 15 Vol. 14 K2.

Page 16. Tracing of a petroglyph of a foot. George Creed - Petroglyphs Nova Scotia Archives MG 15 Vol. 14 K3.

Page 20. Tracing of a petroglyph of a human figure who may be interpreted as Windblower. George Creed - Petroglyphs Nova Scotia Archives MG 15 Vol. 12 E7.

Page 25. Tracing of a petroglyph of that may be interpreted as Kluskap (Glooscap) and the evil Winpe. George Creed - Petroglyphs Nova Scotia Archives MG 15 Vol. 12 E21.

Page 28. Tracing of a petroglyph of a human figure. George Creed - Petroglyphs Nova Scotia Archives MG 15 Vol. 12 E6.

Page 31. Tracing of a petroglyph of a human figure. George Creed - Petroglyphs Nova Scotia Archives MG 15 Vol. 12 E14.

Page 35. Tracing of a petroglyph of two human figures in elaborate ceremonial clothing. George Creed - Petroglyphs Nova Scotia Archives MG 15 Vol. 12 E38.

Page 40. Tracing of a petroglyph of three human figures. George Creed - Petroglyphs Nova Scotia Archives MG 15 Vol. 12 E25.

Page 43. Petroglyph tracing. Nondescript. George Creed - Petroglyphs Nova Scotia Archives MG 15 Vol. 14 L3.

Page 44. Tracing of a petroglyph of two human figures in a canoe lancing fish. Petroglyphs Nova Scotia Archives MG 15 Vol. 12 D13.

Page 62. Tracing of a petroglyph of a snake. George Creed - Petroglyphs Nova Scotia Archives MG 15 Vol. 13-I F9.

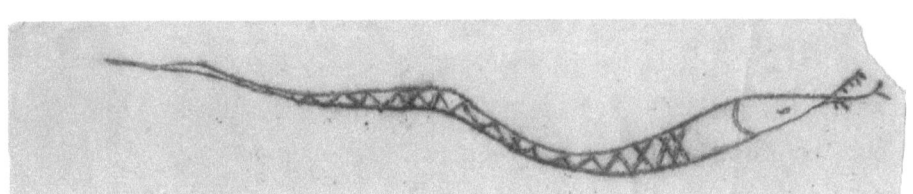

Acknowledgements

To write a book length poem on the most widely known and celebrated character in the Wabanaki oral tradition is to rely on and to acknowledge, above all, the Wabanaki creators of his story: oral and written – remembered, performed, recorded, transcribed, and published. Acknowledging this in spirit is one thing. My bibliography acknowledges it in letter. To recognize the first Indigenous people in northern New England and Eastern Canada is to recognize them as the creators of the first stories.

I acknowledge previous, non-native retellings of the Wabanaki stories, too. Traditional cultures and religions around the world begin with stories, with a universal impulse to retell them. Retellings, interpretations, translations, different form and medium – verbal, musical, visual – lead to variations of a narrative at hand that might be considered primary, which is not necessarily to say original. Focusing on the verbal, translation especially results in variations. There can be numerous translations into different languages as well as copious translations in a single language. Stories from traditional cultures worldwide thrive in such a dynamic, and the most widely known and celebrated character in the Wabanaki storytelling tradition has no less a place within this narrative pantheon.

In *Clooscape the Poet*, he is a storyteller, perhaps, but he tells his own story, the story of himself. It is ostensibly the first story upon which storytellers to come would base their work. *Clooscape the Poet* is a retelling of some of those stories – in his own words. It is a work of fantasy or fiction, suggesting that *they* are the retellings, variations, expansions, translations of the originals that Clooscape, chronologically speaking, was first to conceive of. But by imagining the greatest representative of an Indigenous tradition in the role of creator of his own stories, I would acknowledge and give homage to the myriad who would tell their own stories about him. Thus, he lives on without question.

To write *Clooscape the Poet,* I used Peavey Memorial Library, Bangor Public Library, Ciletti Memorial Library, Pattee Library, Penn State University Libraries, DigitalCommons@UMaine, Grand Manan Museum, Maine Historical Society, Nova Scotia Archives, Nova Scotia Museum of Natural History, Tides Institute & Museum, Sipayik Museum, and Pennsylvania State University. My thanks to all. My gratitude extends to Ken (Bul) Abeles, Ayad Amary, Alexandra Cantalupo, Alicia Cantalupo, Elizabeth Cantalupo Claire, Dana Chevalier, Marianne (Snyder) Close, Tony LaCoute, Philip Krajewski, Roger Lewis, Ngũgĩ wa Thiong'o, Kevin Raye, Donald Soctomah, Dwayne Tomah, and Art Zilleruelo.

Thank you, Public Archives of Nova Scotia, for permission to include petroglyph tracings.

Clooscape the Poet springs from ideas and conversations that, as in most of my writing, I first have had with Barbara Cantalupo, whom I can never thank enough.

Writing a poem like *Clooscape the Poet* would never have dawned on me had we not moved from Bethlehem, Pennsylvania to Muselenk (Moose Island), Eastport, Maine. So, I must thank it, too.

I've been away from the water too long –

And the boats with their lifebuoys
Bright red like poppies.
I've been away from the water too long –

And the sea roses neither invasive
Nor bitter poems.
I've been away from the water too long.

Is it coincidence
Living on Bethlehem's High Street,
Moving to High Street in Eastport,

Plus the historic
Graveyards at the end of both?
I've been away from the water too long

And the tides so steep and strong
On Passamaquoddy Bay.
I want to walk here every dawn.

Writing on the *bellum omnium contra omnes* or the Woodstock Nation, CHARLES CANTALUPO's literary trajectory ranges far: from poems published in religious journals in the 1980s to experimental British and American literary journals in the 90s. Yet the year 2000 marked a new development for Cantalupo with his co-authoring the historic Asmara Declaration on African Languages and Literatures. Writing poetry and literary criticism about Africa and translating poets from Eritrea, he reached a much wider audience than before. This led to his memoir, *Joining Africa* (2012) and returned Cantalupo as a poet to his own American experience. The subtitle, "Further Steps," of one of his subsequent books of poetry could apply to all of his writing. *Clooscape the Poet* takes further steps.

Charles Cantalupo is Distinguished Professor Emeritus of English, Comparative Literature, and African Studies at The Pennsylvania State University. He lives in Eastport, Maine.